CONTENTS

ZENE KAMILI

The Sun Gazing Handbook

Basics, Modern-World Applications, Bio-hacks, Simple Adjuncts & More

COPYRIGHT 2023

Zene Kamili

Front cover image by Zene Kamili

First printing edition 2023

CHAPTER 1: WHY IS THIS A THING?

S un gazing is a very old/ancient practice where one looks at the Sun directly or indirectly to get a desired effect within their body, mind, and beyond. Examples of sun gazing's purposes are stabilizing mental health, feeding directly off sunlight, removing and minimizing excessive toxic energies that we are exposed to in our modern man-made artificial environments, and more.

Sun gazing to improve mental health is very straight-forward when you think about it from a health maintenance standpoint. The human body is like a battery cell. There is a positive (strongly eyes) and negative (strongly feet) polarity. When you take off your shoes (especially rubber sole or nonconductive ones) and stand on natural Earth (especially away from technology and artificial power sources), your feet plug your body into the Earth like a battery, increasing your access to the Sun. This is called grounding. At the bottom of your feet are the beginning of energy meridians. Each portion at the bottom of your feet connect directly to certain parts of your body. Feet are a heavily nervous-dense area in the body, making them highly electrical. If you have foot pain, it may not always be that your feet are hurt. It could be that the painful spot connected to that area is indicating an energy blockage elsewhere in the body (look at a reflexology chart to see the connections). Energy blockages often create pain and inflammation. This could manifest as pain in spots/areas on the sole of the foot (instead of the actual point of aggravation on the body). Grounding increases sun gazing's potential by increasing the body's negative polarity which increases how much sun you can receive, use, and store at one time. Feet ground well but getting into a natural body of water grounds you even more. So, if you are submerged in a natural body of water, you are grounded in a very complete way.

On the other end of that circuit are the eyes. My belief is that a well-grounded body takes some of the strain and responsibility off your eyes, just like it does to inflamed/overworked areas in the body. Seeing is of course taking in light. Eyes, like all other body parts, get use up and need preservation sometimes. Your eyes are just like your feet in that each portion is connected to a certain area in your body. There is an entire very old medical practice called iridology; this practice allows a trained person to look into an individual's eyes and determine poor functioning body parts or areas of health (look at an iridology chart to see how the eyes correspond to other body areas). Eyes are connected to the entire nervous system within the body. When you see light (of any kind), the eyes turn this light into a type of electric current. Artificial light is very different from the Sun, turning the body on in very different (incomplete) ways. The Sun however, has the proper spectrum (think complete diet) of light that the body can convert to the appropriate energies needed to function. Since the Sun is primordial to everything, you don't really need to study its effects to benefit from them. However, artificial light is brand new technology that has been around for an extremely short amount of time. Therefore, it needs to be understood fully prior to using for any lengths of time and should be used very discerningly.

The body is an Earth/Sun energy circuit. Artificial energies in environments get in the way of this energy circuit often, retarding the body from its natural design. When eyes experience the Sun, a whole slew of hormones are produced right in the eyes that maintain the body. Some well-known examples are cortisol, dopamine, melatonin, and vitamin D. There are many hormones made in the eyes from sunshine contact, and the topic has many books that describe and explain it well. The four hormones that I just mentioned are crucial to mental health. For example: cortisol is near the top of the hormone chain's hierarchy; it manages stress and even sleep cycles, dopamine has huge effects on critical thinking and enjoying small pleasures in life, melatonin ensures that your sleep regenerates you to be strong on the next days, and vitamin D affect countless functions from immunity to bone regeneration.

Why do I bring these type of facts up about hormones and light? Much of the world is convinced that the sun is a type of necessary enemy. But what gets overlooked is that the more you don't use the sun, the less you can use it when needed. Yes, I'm saying that if you don't use the Sun, you lose the ability to use the Sun. In regards to sun gazing, if you don't train your eyes (systematically and consistently), you lose your ability to visually convert the sun to resources and energy for the body. I'm saying that an experienced sun gazer has a greater healing/normalizing potential than an inexperienced one because of the body's adaptation with the practice. Same goes for tanning. I'm saying that you need sun gazing in your life. Nevertheless, there are rules and details needed to form a healthy regimen and routine. I write this book to discuss them and learn myself.

Is sun gazing necessary for most people? No, it's not. My opinion/belief is that there is a time and place for it for everyone. For example, if you are a farmer who spends time outdoors for the entirety of daylight's duration, this may not matter much for you because you are living correctly through the responsibilities of your job. If you are considerably limited on the amount of hours you can get outdoors every day, then a consistent systematic sun gazing routine can work wonders for you. If you have issues with mental health or have to think in detail daily, a basic routine will be great for you. I don't believe it is a practice that has to be done consistently over a life time (more on this in chapter 9). This area of knowledge and information (proper amount/frequency) becomes difficult to discern and standardize because the life styles and health of everyone can differ dramatically, even with twins living similar lives. The mainstream is afraid of it. Therefore, I feel that constant self-assessment, judgement, and peer discussions are critical to the success of using this practice. One person may need to use the practice sparingly or periodically but another may need it for years at a time (more on this later).

Sun gazing can be used for protection/mitigation against artificial and toxic environments. When you talk about unnatural modern environments, the usual suspects of the time are likely to come up: blue light toxicity, excessive communication light (radio waves), electromagnetic fields (exudes from any flowing electricity), and artificial surfaces (roads and floor/not the Earth). Each of these categories of toxicity manifest their own specific issues to health. The lack of ability to comprehend, discern, and act on their detriments to the body, often results from these toxicities not necessarily having linear (direct cause/effect) effects on health. For example, blue light disturbs melatonin production but you can disturb this process consistently for months on end and feel just a little bit tired with your productivity less, without you realizing it. Often, medical tests make this obvious and of course a physician may have to explain implications of the results. Unfortunately, unless very experienced, the typical physicians (I think) can't due to lack of specific training; modern day doctors are more drug dealers than problem solvers. Another example in regard to electromagnetic fields is that they affect growth hormone and some say melatonin production. You need tests to track this and you are coupling the test with your/doctor's own subjective analysis. It is easy to attribute one thing to something else and the last place a person often looks is right at home or work. This is where they spend most of their time. Another example is radio waves. Radio waves have slight microwave properties (they are adjacent spectrums of light). Consistently being in a radio wave field subjects you to constant (low scale) dehydration on a cellular level. Hydration is a prerequisite for vitamin D regeneration and sun usage, due to active vitamin D being made in the kidneys. Drinking more water only helps in this case but doesn't fix the situation. A main idea here is the difference between "good light" and "bad light" (most unnatural EMFs are "bad light"). One of my main ideas here is that, adapting to the Sun enhances our recovery from having artificial technology frequencies in our lives.

Though I'm a sun gazing enthusiast, I feel that there is a tremendous depth to it that even I am not willing to explore. During my six years of consistent and extensive practice, I experienced many strange sensations during, immediately after, and while sleep. The majority and most profound ones happened in the first three years for me. Because many of the experiences were beyond usual medical or academic description, I have to label them in blanket terms like spiritual or esoteric. For example, within my first six months of doing it, I experienced what felt like an electric shock into my eyes and body during a fifteen-minute session. My body felt buzzed and deeply full of light and charged for about an hour thereafter. It didn't hurt or anything but it was so weird and unusual that I was simultaneously concerned but amused. In my second year, I experienced seeing colored light oozing out of and trailing people that I encountered. I had this feeling continuously for over six months. Initially, I thought it was overuse of looking at the Sun; however, this experience was distinctly different from that. It felt supernatural because it seemed like I was seeing these people's feelings or something, based on the colors of the light trailing and coming out of them. I loved this sensation but eventually it diminished and ceased. In the middle of my six years, I became very active in my dream life. I remembered most of my dreams, therefore started using the data for self-exploration. Also during the middle to later years, I became very sensitive to all light. I could tell when the Sun was out brightly in the morning no matter where I was. It was like I could see right through my walls. I had to check and self-confirm it many times before actually believing it. Fake light began instantly putting me in poor or peculiar moods. I became very sensitive and empathic around this time, which became annoying because I don't want to always know how other people feel; it can be exhausting.

I learned the most about sun gazing around 2013/14. Astrologically, Jupiter (abundance/huge knowledge and lessons) was heading to my sixth house (health, work, routines). I had some health issues that didn't make sense to me. So, I started exploring the alternative health world. Among others, I found Dr. Jack Kruse (I use a lot of his info to explain ideas here), a super under-rated pioneer in this new age of technology and health. Aside from him, I continued exploring the more obscure world of alternative heath, finding people like Mantak Chia, Hira Ratan Manek, independent YouTubers like Master of Earth, and many others that functioned like a team in helping true fans of alternative health and esoteric knowledge get that under-rated education. Unfortunately, as of now (2023) and nearly much of the past decade, platforms like these have commercialized to the point where this valuable knowledge is buried/diluted/censored. Back then and before, everyone could learn from everyone, of course discerning right or wrong for themselves (my right or wrong isn't necessarily yours).

"Some say that sun gazing originated in India more 2,000 years ago with the teaching of Lord Mahavir of Jain, also known as Mahavira or Vardhamana. However, many civilizations from the Aztecs to the ancient Egyptians practiced sun gazing."(above quote from https://www.thephuketnews.com/feast-on-the-sun-72467.php)

Sun gazing has strong traceable roots into India. A modern day pioneer, the Indian Hira Ratan Manek (12 September 1937–12 March 2022), rediscovered, repackaged, and re-popularized this practice in the new millennia. Through example, he showed a lot of the potential that the human body has with the aid/use of the Sun. He has done many seminars. He is very well-known for extensively practicing and coming up with a protocol that was safe for most people. "Mr. Manek proved that one could gaze at the Sun directly for half an hour if practiced for several months continuously. By the ninth month, the body will become a reservoir of solar energy and can survive without food, he contended." He became famous after demonstrating extensive fasting utilizing the Sun's power. "It was his 211-day fasting at Kozhikode in 1995, that shot Mr. Manek to fame. Later he set a Guinness World Record in 2000 at Ahmedabad, undertaking a 411-day fast, which made him a celebrity across the globe." (above two quotes from this article: https://www.thehindu.com/news/cities/kozhikode/the-man-who-consumed-the-sun-is-no-more/article65219937.ece). H.R.M.'s celebrity led to him supposedly being studied by I.S.R.O (India space research) and N.A.S.A. to make use of his rediscovered knowledge and the application of it.

After discovering Mr. Manek and learning all about him, I became brave enough to actually try the practice. Foolishly, I didn't follow H.R.M.'s protocol properly. I skipped ahead steps (after three months) upon realizing that I could effectively stare at the sun daily for 20-plus minutes; and receive positive results, perceivably without any complications. It just felt natural to me. In later chapters, I'll talk about my regrets, overindulgences, and the consequences of my mistakes. I'll go over approximate timelines so that you can scale my experience to yours. I recommend following the H.R.M. protocol maybe for multiple cycles (3-4 years) before doing some type of more aggressive version.

CHAPTER 2: EYES, THE BODY, AND THE SUN

The Body's Clocks, Rhythms, And Hormones

The body has its own rhythms that it follows over a day. The sun and nature has governs how we should live. However, technology development is interfering with and challenging our abilities to follow these laws. The body has a hormone system that is dependent on environmental and nature's fluxes, a large part of that being the Sun's influence. Let's break down the Sun, body, and its hormone cycles. We could break down many other cycles like cold, rain, seasons, etc. and get different interdependent explanations and results. But, let's just talk about the Sun for now.

A hormone called leptin is now thought to be at the very top of the chain affecting the body on a timely seasonal basis. It is considered the main energy and metabolism hormone. It governs fat storage and overall bodily partitioning of energy. When we get strong Sun regularly, leptin lowers to tell the body there is high food and energy available. Leptin governs just about everything. If you interfere with leptin, for example it getting too high, it affects important lower hormones like insulin. From my understanding, strong Sun or cold temperatures lowers and desensitizes leptin. As I mentioned above, leptin is a master hormone. So if you take a look at it hypothetically, just about any physical health issue can be improved if you begin with improving the things that leptin controls. Learn what leptin controls! Or, just spend a lot of your time in the most appropriate nature for your heredity. Leptin is more seasonal and general but let's talk about less general more day to day hormones.

At the top of the hormone chain, cholesterol is considered a main raw material. Most hormones begin with cholesterol. Whenever there is excessive stress or inflammation in the body, it makes more cholesterol as raw material for more hormones and to repair damage. Sufficient cholesterol in the body is important for this reason. Sun naturally lowers it, if it is too high. 312 nanometer light (UVB) on the skin turns it into vitamin D (WHENEVER I MENTION VITAMIN D BLOOD LEVELS, I'M PURELY TALKING FROM THE SUN/NO PILLS. PILLS ARE GROSSLY INFERIOR AND IN SOME CASES UNPRODUCTIVE).

From cholesterol, the body initially makes pregnenolone, a precursor hormone for most other hormones. Pregnenolone coverts over to cortisol (stress/survival hormone) mainly/firstly. There are many other steroids and other hormones (including vitamin D) that take the leftover precursors from the above mentioned hormones. By this, I mean that if you interfere with it for any reason, it limits all other hormones below it. Naturally, cortisol is high in the morning (wakes you up) and low at night (prep for sleep). It follows the sun. Eating late or too much artificial light at night (anytime actually), raises cortisol higher when it should be lower, preventing melatonin (a sunshine/and cold weather hormone) from releasing fully and repairing your body during sleep. Cold environments (real or artificial) correct many of these hormonal abnormalities.

If you want to critically think on the above paragraph, let's think about this for a moment: cortisol (STRESS HORMONE), because it has preference over the majority of the hormone chain, can steal from all other hormones that make your life fun (even the sunshine vitamin). Though stress is often from real physical irritations and overuses of the body, interpretations of it and psychological stress are regulated by your mind's management of them. I say that to say, don't underestimate the power of mediation, positivity and optimism, and constantly sourcing motivation and inspiration. Make that a priority! You have full control over this part.

For a more detailed and contextual description of the hormone chain, check out this amazing blog: https://jackkruse.com/hormone-cascade-101/?print=print

Feeding The Body With Sun

If you're going to feed your body with the sun (like a food substitute), it'd be good to learn about its schedule of supply and demand. I have taken you through some of the hormonal systems and their hierarchies within the body. Much of these systems are governed by light in nature. Hormones reduce or increase needs for physical food. Over a day's span, the body's hormones follow consistent interdependent cycles. The morning (up to around11 a.m.) is the best time to recharge the body and fill up on the light hormones and energies. The body will have fasted from food and sunlight. Therefore, it will be very receptive and efficient with its storage and use of both. However, if you miss mornings, as close to this time period as you can get is a good secondary plan. Of course, the further you go into the evening, the less effective. At that point, the sunlight is minimizing to darkness to power you down for sleep and regeneration. Usually after sunset, we increase our use of blue light in the home. Blue light stimulates hormones such as cortisol (which should be dropping as night comes) to increase carbohydrate metabolism and reduces melatonin release into the body. Melatonin reduction and blockage decreases your sleep's healing power.

Tanning And Skin Care

The folllowing primarily applies to longterm exposure, not a short vacation. This topic is tricky because, yes, the sun does damage and age skin. However, the damage is short term until the body begins to adapt. Contrary to what many may believe, the damage primarily comes from how you live your life (proper sleep time/duration, poor diet, being in artificial light/energy fields). The Sun will seem like an enemy until you get these type of habits better (sounds like a spiritual guide to me). Many freak out at the first sign of Sun damage and block it any way they can often. Of course, we all are different. Therefore, it's important to scale the use of the information to your level of difference, tolerance, and adaptability.

I myself, have jumped into strong sun without proper prep time (example: relocate for a sunny vacation in the middle of a cold winter). The initial damages that I get always ended up reversing, my skin ending up even better than when I began. These habits, I've been exercising over about a twelve-year span, which is where I started visiting the tropics on a regular basis to observe this.

The ease of the transition that the body makes are based on many factors: skin type, age, amount of time spent in nature, amount of technology and modern conveniences used, diet, sleep, etc. A good preparation method is the use of infrared light. You can do it the artificial way as a last resort but get as much as you can from the sun that you have where you are. In getting infrared light from the sun, early mornings (best) and late evenings are good preparation periods. The closer you are to the equator, the shorter (but stronger) these infrared light dominant periods are. During mid-day, UV (the main healer that people fear) comes in with the infrared light. Why infrared is so good for preparation is because it strengthens, regenerates, and heals the skin and body. It also conditions the skin for stronger shorter wavelength sunlight (UV spectrum). It is also very rejuvenating to mitochondria, which makes water all throughout the body and skin, increasing your tolerances for Sun storage, and reducing signs of aging.

Eat your sunscreen. In a vegetarian diet, loading up on foods from the local rainbow (not foreign foods to your location) gives you the raw material for pigments to properly build and protect your skin. Seaweed is a super under-rated vegetable. It independently thrives in the wild and doesn't need be faked or genetically modified; this decreases the need for hybridization, pesticide use, and artificial cultivation methods. For a non-vegetarian, eggs, seafood (DHA is a major sun protector and anti-inflammatory), and fatty fruit (cholesterol begins the hormone cycle) are excellent. For meat eaters, in the organs and bones are where the bulk of the vitamins and nutrition are, particularly for vitamin A. Vitamin A is really important in how the eyes and the brain deal with light (especially darkness) and is linked to fast acquisition of speech and learning.

Hydration is important but like most other things, hydration tolerance (like eating habits and appetite) takes time and adaptation; you can't do too much too soon, if your body is not ready. Gradually increase your hydration as you would food in your diet. The type of water definitely matters. Get it from a trusted source, for example, without Fluoride added to it. Cold water absorbs faster and better than warm/room temperature water. If you cramp or get weak, consider adding electrolytes and/or more fruit and veggies to your diet.

Fasting And The Sun

You can fast any time but it is easier when you are close to nature. Under cold conditions, you will likely spend much of the time inside under artificial conditions ungrounded (hibernating animals stay grounded). Though hormonally beneficial and facilitated well by the cold, fasting is demanding if you are not hibernating and grounded. When fasting, consider these factors: the less light (or colder weather), the more grounding is beneficial; the more sunlight available, the more the Sun on your surfaces are beneficial; and exercise (you may not feel like doing) and water helps tremendously.

I've noticed the shock of fasting being a little harsh on my skin but it bounces back almost instantly after finishing the fast. Waking early and sleeping early are much more important here because you need to be synched with natural light and dark as best as you can. Fasting isn't just about food; it is more about being in natural light and dark, and focusing on other parts of your noneating life. It also requires conditioning through practice and repetition.

CHAPTER 3: CAN EYES REALLY HANDLE DIRECT SUN?

Red Light

Infrared light is well documented for causing cataracts in the eyes through excessive or improper use. The eyes seem to try to build an extra coating to protect themselves. Since infrared light is a major healer, it increases scar tissue when healing damages in the body. Contrary to IR light ruining the eyes, it has also been well-documented that many eye-diseases can be treated/healed with IR light photo-bio-modulation, specifically the near infrared range. So, from these contradictions as an example, it seems that the use of IR (or any isolated spectrums of light) is very nuanced when trying to use it to treat specific ailments. However, it is important to understand that using infrared light alone versus the full spectrum of the Sun are very different. The Sun is balanced by all the other spectrums/colors, especially the short wavelength purple light (UV). UV and IR light play two very different roles in the body, as do all the other spectrums. I think that it is notable that the extremes of issues come up when scientists isolate and use limited portions of light spectrums and come to full conclusions about the full spectrum light in the Sun.

How much infrared light is in the sun? Approximately 49% of the sun is in the infrared range, 7% in the UV ranges, and less than 1% in the gamma, radio, and x-rays according to https://sos.noaa.gov/. I assume that the remaining 43% percent is in the visible range. According to Dr. Jack Kruse, I humbly paraphrase that the water in the body (80-plus percent) strongly stores infrared light, turning it (cells) into batteries or capacitors. I take that to mean, turn it on to heal and do work. UV light tremendously adds more power to that IR water battery. I bring this up simply to illustrate that light in nature never exist out of a full spectrum, and animals in nature never have to deal with this.

IR light alone is said to cause eye issues but what about if UV was added, just like in sunlight? It changes everything when you consider what UV (particularly UVB) light does. It is a major healer in the body, well known for creating vitamin D, building bones, and super powering the immune system. So, my point here is that the addition of UV to IR (or just full spectrum Sun), in theory, nullifies negative consequences versus using IR light alone. I say all that to say, remove the competing light to supplement your sun gazing/body absorption activities. Even if you use IR light at home for whatever reason, it is important to understand that each spectrum under the umbrella of IR light do specific and different things. It's probably not a good idea to use all or any IR as a fix/cure-all. You have to keep in mind that near-IR, short/mid/far-IR, and ranges in between these take different actions in a body. Although many people play with this with success, this use of light in technology medicine is way ahead of its time and still very experimental.

Ultraviolet Light (Artificial)

The use of UV (in isolation) to heal/supplement is relatively common, even more so in cold regions where sun exposure becomes a luxury. It is often used to heal/treat SAD, to help produce vitamin D, treat psoriasis, etc. Although there is no substitute for the sun, I feel this is definitely a huge step up from using drugs.

I'm going to speak on some of my experiences with supplementing UV from a lamp. Keep in mind that much this is anecdotal. Also, my views and opinions on using them now has change; I am unlikely to do so now. I used them for a span of about a decade. The benefits were greater the younger I was. I first began supplementing UV light when I moved to South Korea from Alabama of the U.S. Korea's sun is weak compared to Alabama's. In the winter for about three months, I used this specialized lamp. At times, I also used it during the rain-season. Through this self-experiment, I learned a lot first-hand about UV light. The first thing that I learned about it was how to use it and get the best results without side-effects. I experimented with the distance that I used it. I found that about two feet away was ideal for me. I gradually increased the time that I used it, initially only doing the recommended two minutes-maximum. The immediate noticeable effect that I would get was a slight increase in heart rate. Another effect that I got was a stimulant caffeine-like sensation that lasted a couple of hours but didn't interfere with me falling asleep. Another effect that I got was more lucid dreams, especially if I used it close to bed time. A year or so later, I began sitting further away (about four feet) and doing ten to twenty minute sessions, getting good results and feeling good. I often read books in front of it, experiencing increased concentration.

Thereafter, I began looking at it with my bare eyes for up to five minutes at a time, experiencing an even greater stimulant-like effect. Over a five-year span, when I would read books in front of it for over fifteen minutes while wearing glasses (glass blocks UV), I got eye injuries; the UV had come through the side of my glasses from an angle (not directly through the lens). This happened three different times over five years. In the injuries, I burned my cornea. The first time this happened, I was really worried that I had ruined my eyes but each time it healed in under two days. The irritation didn't come right away; it was delayed, typically showing up overnight on the next day. I remember waking up in the morning with a lot of mucus on my eyes and them sticking together. When I went outside to sunlight, my field of vision was super bright, unique, and I could see more and different pretty colors than usual (don't get me wrong. I was super paranoid). It felt like what I would imagine lasik eye surgery results to be like. The light was so intense that I wore sunglasses, which I never do for sunlight because I know that they affect the body very unnaturally by altering the natural light coming through the eyes from the sun (inside of buildings, I typically wear blue light-blocking orange glasses). I speak about this not to imply that you try UV light on your eyes (**because it was an accident and I think you should not**!). I mention it to illustrate that I don't think that UV from the natural sun while responsibly sun-gazing will harm any person with normal health. My experiment was far harsher than what you can get through looking at the natural sun.

I played with the use of UV light supplementation over about a decade, which was throughout my thirties. I eventually grew concerned about long-term effects on the skin using this artificial light. Perhaps using it as directed (under two minutes a day) would erase much of the uncertainties of possible risks. With that said, I don't recommend using artificial lights for supplementation extensively (perhaps not at all) or not as directed in the instructions. I no longer use them. I prefer to just accept the limitations of my natural environment or just move to the tropics (consistent strong sun for long hours every day) where this is a nonissue.

Blue Spectrum Light (Artificial)

So, we have talked about the main artificial lights that people use, usually for medicinal/supplemental purposes. Now let's talk about the elephant in the room that everyone sees every day but ignores and have just grown to think that it is harmless. This is a huge topic that many books have been written on already. Blue light is the root of a lot of illnesses. The problem with accepting this is that it is hard to prove, until you pull out statistical data over decades and compare times of increased illnesses alongside changes in the types of lights we use in our respective civilizations. There is a book called The Invisible Rainbow that cleverly traces back over 150 years or so and shows the rises of sickness in correlation to the use of lights, electricity, and technology. The book shows how every time there is a technological advancement, there are subsequent new health crisis that align with the timeframe as well as the regions they were implemented in. However, because of how convenient and useful the advancements are, people easily forget about the problems caused and continue to let the use happen while attributing health issues to other easier targets like food or chemical pollutants.

When you understand that the body and eyes pay attention to **all** (the whole electromagnetic spectrum, even the invisible) light in an environment, constantly adapting to and using it, you have to ask yourself: *can I spend huge portions of my time looking at blue spectrum light (screens and light bulbs) and keep my body exposed to it without consequence?* The use of blue light is so ubiquitous in modern society that most to all people will not acknowledge its detriments or just consider them frivolous. In order for people to see how great the detriments are, timely self-experiments and self-assessments are necessary, but you have to know what signs you are looking for. For example, I learned through taking medical hormone blood tests (DHEA test for example can show how much artificial light exposure is in your life. I learned from Dr. Jack Kruse). I tested in one living environment (about a year) and tested in another living environment (about a year) and saw a huge difference.

So, how am I tying this to sun gazing? As I have shown you above, supplemental UV and IR light are definitely medicines but can also harm you through improper use. Blue light is no different. It does have favorable effects on hormones and can turn the body and brain on, particularly in the morning through the Sun (there is a time, place, and dose for everything). However, just like the UV and IR, its amount of use should be strongly scrutinized, standardized, and used discerningly. These days, it is virtually ignored. Blue light from screens trick the body into thinking that it is noon all of the time. In normal natural life, you only get one chance to see noon per day. If you increase the amount of noons in a day, the body suffers or gets confused. Melatonin (sleep, mitochondrial repair, metabolism) is made from sunlight (particularly UV). Blue light use at night and excessively throughout the day interferes with this. Blue light dehydrates the body (cells) through lowering mitochondrial function (keep in mind that mitochondria make the water in our body and melatonin regenerates mitochondria during sleep). Conversely and counterintuitively, the Sun hydrates the body by increasing mitochondrial function. Aging is a dehydration dependent issue. Blue light is a very strong short wavelength (just like UV) light that has high stimulating power but lacks healing power; UV has both of these and red light regenerates damage. So the question here is: is the UV (in the sun) or the artificial blue light ruining eyes and bodies? I'm pretty sure the answer is somewhere in the middle.

What Science Says About The Eyes' Light Threshold

In referencing this link: http://photobiology.info/

Rozanowska.html let's talk about the thresholds of light by the eyes.

Throughout life, eyes are typically exposed to a flux of 300 (UV) to 1,100 nm (IR) wavelength light. Let's always keep in mind that modern day life has a lot of blue spectrum artificial light. So, I think we should skew these numbers higher to that portion (blue light) more to get an accurate assessment of the average person's light diet. Refer to the picture of the eyeball.

Human Eye Anatomy

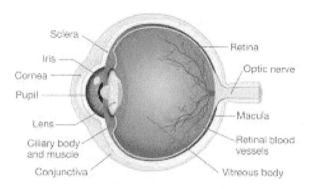

The cornea (outermost film of eyeball) is thought to filter out much of the UV light before it reaches the lens and underlying eyeball (I definitely agree with this because of my above UV light experiment burning my cornea). The cornea is thought to absorb most UVB (below 295 nm – the strongest we usually get naturally) and the lens UVA (above 295 nm – the next strongest we get). The cornea and lens supposedly absorb part of the infrared too, especially the water bands (water strongly absorbs 980, 1,200, 1,430 nm light, all red range. Blue color is the result.). The vitreous gets above 1,400 and the retina gets the visible (390-760 nm) and near IR (760 -1,400 nm). In children, UVA and B reach the retina up to about 8%. By adulthood, less than 1% reaches the retina and by 60, nearly none reaches the retina. (This info may be wrong/off but one can easily shine a UV light into the eye to put this to the test based on whether the person can see it or not – don't try!).

Our typical daily exposures supposedly surpass the daily threshold of what would destroy the retina. Sun gazing is definitely expected to damage retinas based on some of the data in this study. I think it is debateable.

CHAPTER 4:
GROUNDING AND
ITS BASICS

G rounding has been documented to reduce inflammation in the body. Keep in mind that inflammation is swelling in the body that is usually caused by energy blockages or lack of flow. Swelling/inflammation carries a positive (draining) charge. Grounding helps neutralize the positive with the negative charge from the Earth, reducing the blockages of that circuit. It is documented to increase recovery from exercise and daily wear and tear, and reduces blood stickiness.

The skin, hands, feet, and eyes are major conductors of electric energy for the body. The hands and especially the feet are super rich in nerves, and are extremely conducive to energy conduction. The hands and feet are among the most electronegative (energy conductive and absorbing) parts of the body. The further you go away from the hands and feet to the inner body, the more electropositive (energy consuming). They seem to be designed to take energy from the outside in to feed the body's more inward portion.

So, when you connect organically to the natural Earth, a

tree, swim in a lake, etc., you are neutralizing energy blockages and giving your body access to free energy. However, we don't do this nearly as much as we should, adding limits to the body's function. I'm now going to talk about what grounding is, isn't, and elaborate on more of its significances.

Grounding On Artificial Or Natural Surfaces

A modern day human constantly gets neutralized away from the healing power of the Sun through being ungrounded. Grounding's concept is simple but a little misunderstood. In order to appreciate the effects and significance of grounding, one must realize how much we are not grounded over a day or a life time. Most houses are built with a foundation of material that don't conduct the negative energy from the Earth well, if not at all. So every night we sleep, the body misses the healing power of this negative energy; it dilutes the healing power of sleep. Next, we wear shoes most of the day. Shoes (particularly rubber soles) block the conduction of the Earth's energy from entering us when we walk around. Blacktop or tar roadways typically have chemicals in it that block electric energy conduction. However, more natural material, like rock or cement have conducting abilities, particularly if the lower layer is cement or rock also.

So when you consider that modern life has blocked us from much of the negative energy/electricity, getting this energy from the Earth becomes a conscious responsibility. Blocking us from the Earth's energy is becoming the way and the standard of the modern world. Much of our absorption of and ability to use light (the skin or eyes) is guided by how electrically excited the body becomes when it encounters light. Grounding neutralizes this excitation, allowing more of the sun's power (think of it as positive energy) to do its healing. A genetically lower light-absorbing body would especially benefit if they are plugged into the Earth's energy through grounding. The Earth's pole regions have the highest grounding power while the latitudes closer to the equator have less grounding power but higher sun power. Grounding is the other side of this Earth to Sun energy dynamo. They go hand and hand. Genetics and ancestry play a large role in knowing what area on Earth gives you the most appropriate ratio of Sun to Earth energy. A DNA test for genetic lineage may prove helpful in figuring this out for you specifically. Really, the take home message here is to dedicate some time every day to being in a completely natural environment as naked as you can legally/comfortably be and ground yourself.

Water And Grounding

Unlike grounding with your hands and feet, being in a body of water grounds the entire body, plus has other added benefits. Aside from water being more conductive than surfaces, its makeup and qualities are superior in energy conduction and connection. It also interacts with the body in special ways due to it being a crystal.

In regards to grounding and blocking EMFs, bodies of water are one of the best options out there. Water is like a faraday cage, in that it shields you from electrostatic and electromagnetic influences. Water is like a flowing crystal. Crystals transfer energy very well. Water in the natural Earth connect to its negative electricity and connects you to that energy's conductive power. Since a person is almost all water, you basically become that body of water and acquire those positive qualities. Although you are in a house (that is likely not grounded), when you take a shower or bath, you get the grounded effect for the duration of your shower. Jumping in a river also gives you a long lasting refreshing feeling that you may attribute solely to an adrenaline rush but I'm sure that it is the positive (bad ones) electrostatic being neutralized, resetting you.

Another aspect of water that favorably affect the body is

its temperature. We will go more in depth on this in the next chapter solely dedicated to using cold temperatures to heal or get fit. Keeping in mind that water is a type of malleable crystal, the lower the temperature of the water, the more crystalline (organized and energy conductive) it becomes. In order for water to become ice in stages, it has to absorb energy to organize. Cold water is very high energy in comparison to warmer. In order for the water to get cold, it has to get of rid any energy-draining impurities that oppose its transition to ice. Drinking ice cold water is definitely an energetically favorable move. Getting into a cold body of water (the colder the better to an extent) organizes the water in you, making your body become more of a crystal, helping you to block out bad radiation effects from your environment.

Combining water and sun gazing is a power move. Water has certain bands of light that it favorably absorbs such as the infrared range (particularly the water bands mentioned earlier). All the above mentioned aspects of water come into play when you sun gaze from water. Cold water requires more organization; it uses more UV light (high powered light) energy to organize. Keep in mind that organization takes energy to become order. My assumption is that this is part of the positive affect gained from utilizing cold water to enhance your sun gazing experience.

Grounding During Sleep

As mentioned above, the typical modern house is built in such a way with material that block you from grounding to the Earth. If you have dirt or cement floors on ground level, you are probably fine. If you live in a building floors up, you are probably not. One method that I experimented with while living in an apartment in a city was to ground my bed from outside. I did this by connecting an insulated wire to my bed and connecting the other end to a metal pole stuck in the ground outdoors. I learned from a very important documentary that I found on YouTube about a family living in high latitude snowy Canada learning that they could greatly improve their sleep and reduce inflammation, relieving them of a lot of their mystery health issues.

There are a lot of inventions (such as grounded bed sheets and mats) that claim to ground you properly in a modern home. These inventions connect to the power grid, which becomes tricky if you don't know exactly how the electrical system is connected in your building. It is possible that they can draw artificial electricity to you from other sources. I'd use these with extreme caution with the understanding that the technology and power systems are continually being changed. I think that grounding your bed sheet directly to Earth is the simplest way and takes away the guess work but even with that, you don't want to ground over Earth loaded with buried electrical conducting wires or machines. *To ground your bedsheet directly to the Earth, you simply get a metal pole, drill it into the ground, and connect a wire from it to your bed.*

Grounding is a very simple concept but it is boggles the mind how something so easy could require a manual to correctly do. The modern world needs manuals to keep up with the effects of human creations. Camping in nature or your own backyard is always a fun, simple, and refreshing option to get your healing Energy from the Earth as you sleep.

CHAPTER 5: COLD ADAPTATION, HOW, AND WHY

C old adaptation brings out some of the best qualities in the human body. Some people have favorable genetic dispositions (DNA compatibility and ancestry) to this and handle it far better than others. Yet and still, anyone can transform their body, mind, and health by implementing it into their life at their own personal scale. I am very dark in complexion (equatorial dominant ancestry) and can easily endure 40-plus minute full body ice baths happily. I love them. My own personal theory (based on nothing) is that we all share a lot of the same DNA, just waiting to be expressed when we put ourselves in the right conditions. Like a lock in the key, we get a specific reaction. For example: in exposure to excessive heat, the body makes what are called heat-shock proteins, which favorably make the body get strong in various other ways than just enduring high heat.

I've rudimentarily talked about some of the effects of cold above on water's chemistry and physical interactions with the body. In having a better understanding of that, a lot of it overlaps into cold adaptation practice and training.

What Does It Do?

I'm going to use a lot of Jack Kruse's theory here to support my explanation. He ties disparate knowledge together superbly into coherent unified theories. Firstly, cold water is an advanced faraday cage in that it protects the body from unproductive electrostatic energies, allowing it to do its normal function at higher levels.

Acute exposures (versus chronic) are well-known to be powerful anti-inflammatories. When you get an injury and swelling, you are usually instructed to put ice on it to relieve the swelling. Inflammation's polarity is positive (energy using/losing) and there is a lot of chaos there. Adding ice promotes order and organization, allowing energy to come to that area and order it much easier. Now, consider if you did that to the entire body. The body would become more organized and ordered, which would speed up its healing modalities. Now, consider if you had the adaptability to endure longer sessions; then you would get longer sessions of healing. So, the amount of healing that you'd get from your sessions would be dependent on how long your adaptation allows you to.

The length of and healing power of your sessions would be strongly influence by the strength and adaptability of your mitochondria. Mitochondria are the most basic way the body (cells) make energy. Mitochondria are adaptable in what they can tolerate and produce. They are a source of power for the body as well as tolerance for changing environments and more. When you exercise, you increase the power of your mitochondria in specific and selective ways, whether that be for endurance or strength and power; there is genetic variability there. As for cold environments (or hot ones), mitochondria have to make adaptations just the same as for fitness. In a cold environment, mitochondria have to increase the amount of heat that they make to keep the body warm to maintain homeostasis and stay alive. So when mitochondria increase the body's ability to make heat, it increases its overall fitness of them to do all other functions collaterally. So, you trained to make more heat but you also trained every other thing that mitochondria are fit and responsible for.

Humans screw their bodies up by going against the grain of what nature wants them to do. In an oversimplified sense, we are here to move through our environments, following the influences of the Sun and weather. If we were to do that, we'd get exercise, eat nearby local food, get consistent light on the body, sleep systematically, etc.; this would all alter based on where we were on Earth. However, we don't do that, and the result is our hormones trying to give the wrong signals at the wrong times (chaos and disorder). The brain constantly makes assessments of how much light it sees and the temperature. This tells the body what to slow down/speed up. Dr. Kruse says (and I paraphrase) that it results in an inflammatory problem in the brain (with the master hormone leptin) where it can longer take proper account for light cycles and seasons. Cold can relieve, desensitize, and reset the body to account for its environment again. Collaterally, a lot of the body becomes desensitized and you feel a lot of what you weren't feeling before (emotions, appetite/taste, touch, etc.).

Who Benefits

Modern living people benefit most. Cold adaptation is a way to right many of the wrongs done when we divorce from nature. It is like a reset button. If you can feel and react (through the brain) the environmental cues, the body automatically does what it is supposed to do. When you can't innately pick these things up, then you can't listen to your body. In my belief, you inhabit a body that reacts to nature but listens to you; sometimes if your decisions are too bad, then it blocks/removes you from making decisions.

If you have an illness or low functioning body, sometimes it could very well be inflamed. Inflammation is a block in energy conduction. Making the body more crystalline and efficient through acute temperature change can change your whole bodies function, mood, and outlook on life. Though you may not solve the root problem, you could take the strain off the entire body enough for it to figure it out on its own. There are many hormonal effects of cold adaptation. One major one is the increase in melatonin production (the sleep and regeneration hormone and mitochondria maintenance); this is a sign that winters (very cold ones in particular) are maybe meant for sleep, regenerating, and resetting the body. It is probably not smart to miss the majority of a winter inside under artificial conditions. I always make a point in life to embrace at least a little bit of suffering every single day. Sometimes, I'd swim in the ocean at 0 degrees (a couple of minutes); granted, I systematically trained to be able to do so. Even if you don't like your environments factors, try and master (or play) the hand that you are dealt or just move someplace else. Mental health and immunity are definitely maintained through embracing the cold or training for the adaptation. If it is cold already where you are, just simply do more outdoor stuff. If you live in a tropical paradise, the cold can make your whole experience a euphoria.

How To Cold Adapt At Home

Cold adaptation at home is pretty straight-forward. Nevertheless, many people are confused or intimidated by it. I completely understand because I've been there. There have been many blogs or podcasts written on how to do so. However, I will explain my way as I think that my way makes the transition painless, systematic, and easy.

At home you need a bucket (or huge garbage can) that you

can fit your whole body into comfortably. You need a freezer that you can freeze and store about forty liters (two liter bottles each) of ice bottles in. Your bucket needs to be in a place where you can fill it and empty the water rather easily. This can be in a large bathroom or outside near a water faucet.

First you fill your bucket with room temperature water. Get inside of it and do your first session for about fifteen to twenty minutes. This should not be a problem at all. After you get out of the water and you feel chilly or cold, it should take forty minutes-maximum for your body to go completely back to normal. If this is the case, then you are ready to move on to the next step.

As for breathing, it is really important for a beginner (or a person having difficulty) to focus on it. So, here are ways to do so. Breath in and out through the nose. Take long deep breaths. Really put your mind into your breathing; imagine the air flowing into you all the way through your body and back out. Make it a meditative session. This really helps with the time and takes your mind off of the more intense sessions. When you no longer have to focus on your breathing, then I recommend listening to a good podcast or music to really enjoy your time or multi-task. Some people believe in mouth breathing but my belief is that it subconsciously makes the body panic. So, experiment on your own to find your way.

After you've mastered the bucket of room temperature water, bring only one bottle (two-liter) into the water with you for the next session. There should be nearly no change. It should still take forty minutes-maximum for your body go completely back to normal after you get out. If it takes a little longer than this, repeat the process for another session or more until it does.

Once you are able to do the last step and recover within forty minutes, add another water bottle and repeat the process. Every session thereafter, following the same guidelines (keep adding one bottle every session or two). You can do sessions everyday if you are aggressively trying to change something. Or, you can do every other day. I think if you take more than two days off between sessions, then your adaptions will be very slow.

It is important to understand that this activity is similar to a progressive strength/endurance building exercise routine. You have to stay consistent but if you miss too many sessions, you may have to scale back your ice bottles and start over. Think of the ice bottle as weights on an exercise bar; you build your ability over time.

If you are consistent, then you should be doing a full bucket of ice for twenty-minute sessions in three weeks to three months maximum (depending on how healthy/adaptive you were to begin). I almost forgot to mention, **get in the water first and add ice bottles after**. The water chilling will be slow and gradual over about five minutes versus already at its coldest.

When the temperature outside drops under about fifty degrees Fahrenheit, I'd scale back on my frequency. Or, begin swimming outside in a river, ocean, or natural body of water (do half your usual time until you're confident. When the outdoor temperature drops to under forty degrees Fahrenheit, I'd stop the sessions and just begin spending more time doing outdoor activities. In the forty-degree and under outdoor temperature range, natural bodies of water are a huge step up from the ice tubs (the difficulty increases significantly). At this point, natural bodies of water will begin to become risky and you will need a person with you just in case. I recommend referring to someone more specialized in how to do the outdoor cold training to guide you with this. With outdoor training, the same rules apply: it should take you about forty minutes for your body and temperature to return back to normal. When I did winter outdoor sessions, I typically had a nice meal waiting to heat me back up quickly.

As for eating, if you are really sensitive to the cold, eating a good meal before a session is probably best until you begin getting the hang of things. I always did my sessions first thing in the morning on an empty stomach. Sometimes, I'd do forty-degree ocean swims for fifteen minutes after work around five pm. This is highly dependent on the person but it's probably smarter to try after eating meal first and change later after you feel comfortable.

CHAPTER 6: SUPPLEMENTS - MY TOP PICKS AND WHY

Colloidal Gold

C olloidal gold is a supplement that you can easily buy or make yourself at home with distilled water, Himalayan pink salt, sodium citrate, and an electricity generator (about $100/takes twenty minutes to make) or a smaller much slower one (about $30 and takes a day or more to make). When you make it at home, you basically add strong electrolytes to pure water and send electricity through an electrode clipped to gold into the water, resulting in atomic-size gold electric particles forming a new gold compound that the body can utilize for nutrition. You use a parts-per-million device to test the water before and after to calculate how much gold accumulated in your water. The more gold accumulates, it results in the water becoming pink (less gold nanoparticles) to red to dark purple (a lot of gold). You can make a two-month supply in one session. Here's my YouTube video for making it at home: https://

www.youtube.com/watch?v=Qiv1i1HTW60

I will talk about my anecdotal experience and give my own observation first. I'll end by giving the information that you will likely encounter when you look this up through common information and sales channels. I have about of a year of non-stop experience supplementing with colloidal gold. Colloidal gold is actually the inferior version of monatomic gold, which is more difficult to make and come by for the commoner. When you take it, it does not feel drug-like; it feels very natural as if it opens doors that you naturally just don't keep open. My first few months of experience supplementing this were dramatic. It added another layer to my mind/consciousness. What I mean by this is that I became (more) aware of other parts of my own perception (think multiple personalities/existences for reference). So, it was like I had extra help thinking and doing things (it was completely a cooperative feeling). As those first months passed, those minds gradually began merging, making concentration excellent. I began really enjoying my own companionship and mental well-being. It became easier to do task that required sustained mental effort over hours. Its use facilitated a carefree easy-going attitude that promoted the feeling that everything was going to be alright; it promoted optimism. As for my skin and looks, I did see slight improvements initially but nothing to brag about like I got from the mental effects. My dreams became much more memorable and lucid; I don't recall this effect diminishing much until about six months in. At the point of beginning supplementation with this, I was beginning my sixth year of dedicated (twenty minutes a day average) sun gazing. For reasons that I will discuss in the next chapter, I stopped sun-gazing with consistency (sometimes doing brief sessions on whims). Supplementing colloidal gold seemed to give me the pick-me-up that I was missing from no longer sun gazing. By then, sun gazing for me had become addictive and routine; colloidal gold made it not feel like an addiction, diminishing my reliance on it. I really enjoyed being in the Sun while supplementing it; it made a little bit of Sun go a long way for me mentally. That's my raw anecdotal experience with it. Now, let's talk about what you commonly read and watch about this supplement.

If you want to deep dive on the details (colloidal silver and platinum included), I recommend Wikipedia first and from there look at some of the ads on Etsy (metaphysically rich info but not academic), and check out the detailed (monotonous) studies in medical journals. However, for my quick convenient purposes here, I'm showing you below a modified excerpt from an article telling about why common people take this supplement. It is from https://active-silver.co.uk/blogs/blog/3-reasons-to-use-colloidal-gold

"(Begin modified excerpt) Colloidal gold is very similar to colloidal silver and is produced in the same way. Colloidal gold and silver consist of nanoparticles of precious metals suspended in distilled water. The nanoparticles are almost weightless, preventing sediment from accumulating at the bottom of the container and allowing for even distribution.

Here are three reasons to use colloidal gold. As for skin health, it is known to have benefits when maintaining or repairing skin. It is thought to aid with cellular activation and rejuvenation. Many use colloidal gold orally and topically to feed the cells and increase the likelihood of healing. It is known for its anti-inflammatory and anti-ageing properties, making it ideal for those who would like optimal skin health. As for mood, there are reports suggesting that colloidal gold may help to improve mood and may have benefits for those who suffer from anxiety, depression and alike. More studies need to be carried out on this but signs may be promising regarding colloidal gold and mood. In regards to brain health, colloidal gold is known to be a stimulant for the cells in our body, it may help with cognitive function. Nerve cells carry electrical signals in the brain and with increased stimulation, a higher level of brain function may be achieved. This can then lead to higher levels of concentration and better mental alertness (end modified article excerpt)."

Colloidal Silver

Colloidal silver is another supplement that you can easily buy or make at home. It is even easier and quicker to make than the gold. All you need is an electricity source (like with the gold above) and baking soda (or sodium citrate, like above). You know it is discharging and entering the water from its pale yellow (small amount) to deep amber/urine color (higher concentrated amount). It takes about ten minutes to make a two-month supply (using the above voltage generator method).

I'll follow the same pattern as above, giving my own anecdotal experiences and thoughts, followed by the common information that you find in searches and information channels. I supplemented the silver about four months after beginning the gold. Unlike the gold, it didn't give me instant and clear mental sensations, although it did noticeably alter my dream life to complement the effects of the gold. Also unlike the gold, supplementing this too close to bedtime sometimes (not all of the times) resulted in a stimulated effect that excited my mind from immediately sleeping. I supplemented the silver for its purported anti-bacterial/viral/fungal effects. I was aware of its reputation for turning people blue (people that consumed irresponsible amounts of the improperly made version). So, I kept my doses modest but not low. The biggest effect that I noticed from taking this is that after about six months, my completely ruined toe nail (athletes foot) had begun growing back in a regular pattern. About a year after supplementing, my nail had fully regrown. Keep in mind this nail had been ruined for a decade or more and I thought it would never fix naturally. As for keeping me from getting contagions, I don't know if it protected me from that. However, like much of my life, I've resisted well against most all contagious sicknesses.

As I did with the colloidal gold, here is a modified excerpt that talks about why the average user supplements colloidal silver. It is from: https://www.medicalnewstoday.com/articles/324793#how-does-it-work.

"(Begin modified excerpt) Colloidal silver is popular as a natural remedy, though no research supports its use. Many websites and news outlets claim that colloidal silver has a range of health benefits, including the ability to prevent certain diseases. However, because there has been so little research, it is not clear whether it has these effects. Some people use colloidal silver as a natural remedy. The purported benefits include: cleansing the gut, boosting the immune system, treating fungal infections, improving skin health, and preventing the flu/shingles/herpes/certain types of cancer. Because of the lack of evidence, in 1999 the FDA ruled that products containing colloidal silver could not claim to be safe or effective. According to the NCCIHT, there are no known benefits to taking silver orally, and it is not an essential nutrient for the body. Silver does have some medical uses. It is an effective antimicrobial when applied to a person's skin, meaning that it can kill harmful microbes. This is why some manufacturers use silver in their bandages. However, little evidence suggests that taking it orally has any benefit to humans. Here's how it works. Silver can kill microorganisms by binding to their cells, without necessarily damaging human cells. Researchers are still looking into the mechanisms behind silver's antimicrobial properties. However, there is no evidence that colloidal silver has beneficial antimicrobial effects when ingested by mouth (end modified excerpt).

Colloidal Platinum

Colloidal platinum is made just like the gold (see above). The difference is that the water doesn't change color, it stays clear. You have to depend on the parts-per-million meter to know what you are/not getting. Here is my YouTube video for making it: https://www.youtube.com/watch?v=wwh_RhmMU0Q

In following the same pattern as the above gold and silver, I'll share my anecdote followed by more objective information. I supplemented the platinum about six months after beginning the gold. Unlike the silver, the mental effects were clearly apparent and discernable. Mentally, I got this added layer of intense focus. It was not drug-like at all; it felt like something that I knew I was capable of feeling and doing that finally showed up. So, it felt distinctly different but not really was a surprise or anything. Like the gold, the effect gradually melded into one feeling over a few months. Reading became more focused, precise, and deliberate. What became really apparent was its effect on my nervous system when I exercised. I progressively train usually and often tried to beat my previous performances. Within a couple of weeks of use, I could do a lot more repetitions for difficult callisthenic exercises such as the nordic hamstring curl (very difficult slow progressing exercise for most people). I increased the repetitions so high in a short period of time that a hamstring injury resulted (but recovery was speedy). My daily runs for six-plus miles consisted of frequent personal bests despite the heavy frequent schedule. These performances continued to improve over many months. I think that had I not had my exercise schedule as a platform to measure the effects, I would not be able to see and appreciate how great of a recovery aid this supplement is. As I did with the gold and silver, here is a modified excerpt from a commercial article that gives their take on it from a common/more conservative perspective. It is from https://www.colloidalsilverzone.com/

colloidal-platinum-benefits/.

> "(Begin modified excerpt) If you love to work out, especially rigorous ones, then the colloidal platinum is very beneficial. It ensures that there is a healthy tissue regeneration in your body. This supplement is believed to increase the electrical transmission that goes on in the synapses of your brain, this promotes the regeneration of the neurological tissues. Platinum also increases your level of libido as an individual. It can improve mental focus and creativity. Platinum helps to resist attacks on the body's immune system. It is very integral for skincare.

> It has been shown to exhibit antioxidant activity, reduce inflammation and protect the skin layer especially the outer one; ultimately this leads to a stronger, clearer, healthier and more beautiful skin. Colloidal platinum is useful in health circles. Drugs containing platinum are used to treat prostate and ovarian cancers. Now, it can even be used to diagnose treat cure or prevent other forms of the disease. Several types of frequently used chemotherapy drugs have platinum nanoparticles as its major ingredient, just as stated by the food and drug administration (end modified excerpt)."

As for all the above colloidal supplements that I've talked about above, they are hard to sum up in a clear worded explanation. But as a general quick reference, I'd say that gold unifies your awareness and calms an overwhelmed mind, silver speeds your nervous system for pathogen elimination, and platinum increases the power that you focus on to get things done and recover. Keep in mind that all of this information is for informational purposes and aren't meant to be health advice at all.

Do your own thorough research as I have done to apply things to yourself.

Wine

Wine is a tricky one because it is drug-like. There are definitely levels to the types and qualities of wine that you buy. Wine works best under strong sun. The weaker the sun, the more toxic wine's effects become in my opinion. The grape has some amazing properties and track record. Much of its health facilitating effects are related to its photosynthetic relationship. I'll talk about that at the end. From here, I'll follow the same format as above in talking about its positivity under responsible consumption.

I have about a decade of consistent and inconsistent winc drinking. I appreciate it a lot more in my older age, especially because it is the only alcohol that I tolerate well now. My opinions here about wine will be mostly about the medicine-like effects that I've received from it.

Socially, I love a glass of wine, especially with some good Sun, and some good company; it is just a consistent smooth happiness for me. As for mental performance, I have found wine to dramatically increase my inner awareness and contentment, especially while doing a difficult or frustratingly draining task (especially of an academic or social nature). My mind loses much of its rigidity and accesses a lot of creative pathways giving me a heavy flow of momentum, allowing a lot to be done under circumstances where I feel very stuck. The following day, I feel refreshed mentally and physically (when I don't overdo it). It operates very much like a supplement in me versus the alcohol that it is. It is easy to abuse for me because how smooth and helpful that it is.

In regards to fitness, I have used wine for over a decade as a go-to food for recovery, especially from hour-plus endurance exercise sessions. Many times in preparing for full and half marathons, I was able to progressively train, fully recovering day by day. I consumed it (1/3 to a full bottle) after workouts, along with quality balanced meals, on an every-other-day basis. My meals would be fully digested when I wake and I'd be fully ready to run heavy mileage on the next morning or evening. There is a lot of data out there about why wine is a decent recovery aid such as its polyphenol content and its effects on mitochondria. I know that it sounds like I am promoting something that most would say you shouldn't but this is one of those things that either works amazingly or it doesn't.

The following information is from Dr. Jack Kruse via a Facebook post; it is modified for my convenience. Because the internet is loaded with information on the health benefits of wine, I will just use this link because of the uniqueness of its perspective. It is from https://m.facebook.com/drjackkruse/photos/a.568822376515454/2824707710926898/

> "(Begin modified excerpt) So if you had to make a choice between coffee and wine as a health beverage what would be your first choice? Think about it. Why does one or two glasses of red wine high in resveratrol seem to help health when it is studied? Did you know resveratrol is a fluorophore chemical? That means its electrons absorb sunlight at 312 nm range. This means the chemical made naturally by grapes absorb UV light in a way to help refill cells with this regenerating frequency without causing any damage that "worries" the conventional dermatologists. This chemical effectively binds sunlight and water to make a super UV cocktail that increases the DC electric current. Even though there is a small amount of alcohol in the wine, the benefits far outweigh the risk for most people. Do you know what else resveratrol can do that coffee cannot do? It can improve your vitamin D level by altering your Vitamin D receptor. This is why I tend to drink

wines from the Andes mountains at high elevation whose grapes are bathing in UV light 24/7. Resveratrol powers up your immune system in ways few people ever realize unless they become a MITOCHONDRIAC (a mitochondrial performance enthusiast)!!!! (end modified excerpt)"

Spirilina

I have spirulina here because it is a super green food. It's in the supplement category because it takes a lot/special preparation or processing to be served as food. The nutrition is very complete and it's usually from natural sea origins. Most buy it in powder or pill form. The quality varies greatly and you have to do your homework on it before sourcing. Sea vegetables are a wise long-term source of nutrition compared to land vegetables because they are one of the only foods now that don't need to be genetically modified. The issue that I'm making here with genetic modification is that GMO foods are weaker genetically, therefore photo-synthetically, to non-GMO foods. The obvious proof is in that GMO foods need very careful maintenance to survive in nature such as more pesticides, hybridization, and they easily get over-grown by other plants. Spirulina (and sea vegetables in general) are very independent, indicating a natural bond with nature and strong genes for survival that give that same information to your body when you consume it.

It may not be that tasty to many but if you play with it on certain dishes, you can make some really unique delicious dishes that you grow to crave. One of my favorite ways to serve it is to include a modest amount of powder to soup-like dishes that have combine boiled orange-colored vegetables with a highly cooked mushy starch like rice, flavored with salt, fish, or meat. It is a nutrition and chlorophyll-dense green food that is compatible with most environments and prepares you well for the sun. Here is a modified excerpt from: https://www.ncbi.nlm.nih.gov/pmc/articles/PMC3136577/

"(Begin modified excerpt) Spirulina is a microscopic and filamentous cyanobacterium that derives its name from the spiral or helical nature of its filaments. It has a long history of use as food and it has been reported that it has been used during the Aztec civilization. Spirulina refers to the dried biomass of Arthrospira platensis, an oxygenic photosynthetic bacterium found worldwide in fresh and marine waters. This alga represents an important staple diet in humans and has been used as a source of protein and vitamin supplement in humans without any significant side-effects. Apart from the high (up to 70%) content of protein, it also contains vitamins, especially B12 and provitamin A (β-carotenes), and minerals, especially iron. It is also rich in phenolic acids, tocopherols and γ-linolenic acid. Spirulina lacks cellulose cell walls and therefore it can be easily digested.

Many toxicological studies have proven *Spirulina's* safety. *Spirulina* now belongs to the substances that are listed by the US Food and Drug Administration under the category Generally Recognized as Safe (GRAS). *Spirulina* is relatively easy to cultivate but flourishes only in alkaline lakes with an extremely high pH and in large outdoor ponds under controlled conditions. There are only a few areas worldwide that have the ideal sunny climate for production of this alga, including Greece (Nigrita, Serres), Japan, India, United States and Spain. Currently, *Spirulina* can be found in health food stores and is sold mainly as a dietary supplement in the form of health drinks or tablets. Microalgae have been used for more than 10 years as dietary supplements without significant side-effects (end modified excerpt)."

Herbs Known To Rebuild Eyes And Vision

Bilbery

Bilberries can be eaten fresh or dried, as a tea, or standardized into and extract to a concentration of maybe 25%. Anthocyanins are believed to be the most potent nutrient responsible for repairing and supporting the retina and vision.

According to Mountsinai health library's website:

(Begin modified excerpt) Anthocyanosides found in bilberry fruits may be useful for people with vision problems. During World War II, Britissh fighter pilots reported improved nighttime vision after eating bilberry jam. Studies have shown mixed results, however, bilberry has been suggested as a treatment for retinopathy (damage to the retina) because anthocyanosides appear to help protect the retina.

Although thought to be generally safe, eating excessive leaves or extracts can become problematic. As with any herb or self self treatment, it'd be wise to consult with a trained herbalist or specialist prior to implementing this as a self treatment or supplement.

Eyebright

Here is an excerpt from Peacehealth.org on Eyebright:

(Begin modified excerpt) Traditionally, a compress made from a decoction of eyebright is used to give relief from redness, swelling, and visual disturbances due to eye infections. A tea is sometimes given internally along with

topical treatment.

Here is a modified excerpt from Healthline:

(Begin modified excerpt) It contains several beneficial plant compounds such as luteolin and quercitin, which mimic antihistamine drug actions. Contains compound labeled iridoids, which was found through studies to minimize heart scarring after a heart attack, retaining some of its healthy functioning. Studies shown that most participants were relieved of minor eye irritations, inflammation, and swelling in 1 -2 weeks of use. It's used in teas, extracts, eye drops, and more for treatment.

Essential Foods & Vitamins For Vision-Building And Maintenance

The following foods and the above herbal supplements, I suggest creating a smoothie/shake to consume daily to regularly to support or build your eyes and vision. I'm pointing out specific nutrients but promote whole foods first and primarily (if so, take together). Whole foods should always be first. Shortcutting pills and supplements alien in nature is misleading. Take the time and master combing whole to master the essence and tastes of smoothy combinations, stir fry meals, and medicinally combining whole food to taste good while making you feel good. Really enjoy the experience. Ultimately, it is why we are here.

Alpha Lipoic Acid

The body make this naturally, it's rich in meat, and is a very potent antioxidant. Is both water and fat soluble; I guess you could say it is works short (water) and long (fat) term in the body. It rejuvenates other type antioxidants in the body. It chelates and detoxifies the body. It is really good for supporting nerve damage (such as with diabetics). Eyes are full of nerves and polyphenol built components. Its effect on nerves is its biggest point of focus in my point of view here. This nutrient is not abundant in a natural diet. If this a focus of yours, supplementing may be a good option (if supplement, r-alpha lipoic acid, not the (s) version, is said to be the potent one). Here are a few vegetarian foods that are particularly higher than most other foods: spinach, broccoli, brussel sprouts, tomatoes.

Quercetin

The flavanoid quercetin is one the best natural antihistamines and anti-inflammatory. It's a great blood thinner (blood flow great for eyes) and cleaner. Quercetin has an endless list of benefits that ultimately tie back to outstanding vision health. According to Rebuildyourvision.com:

> *(Begin modified excerpt) Consuming quercetin is a great way to enhance vision and prevent cataracts. It has been shown to clean up cataracts (which is a protein buildup on the eye lens). It has been shown to prevent the buildup of aldose reductase, an enzyme common to diabetics that buildup on the lens, cornea, and retina.*

Some common quercetin rich vegetarian foods are: Onion (red especially), apples (peel especially), capers, radish leaves, capers,

Vitamin A

This is well-known for helping night vision, cataracts, dry eyes, cataracts, macular degeneration. It is fat soluble (stores well in the bodyfat). It is a component of rhodopsin proteins which allows one to see in low light conditions and have overall better vision. It is intimately involved in keeping the eyes lubricated. Vitamin A has been studied and associated with learning, memory, and the acquisition of speech; I say this to say it is a nutrient that goes far beyond just eyes and vision.

Rich vitamin A vegetarian food: Orange colored whole foods, green leafy veggies, squash

Vitamin C

This vitamin is very important in general health, is a great antioxidants, and plays key roles in regeneration involving collagen and blood vessels. It's water soluble (doesn't stick around in the body too long). It works very synergistically with many of the nutrients/foods on this list, enhancing the purposes for supplementing. Vitamin C lowers in the eye as we age, reducing the antioxidant protection, vessel building nutrition that it is most well-known for. According to Medical News Today, a 10-year longitudinal study of around 1,000 twins indicated that there was a 33% increase in cataract protection, them overall having clearer lenses.

Some vegetarian foods rich in Vitamin C: Citrus fruit, broccoli, brussel sprouts, and berries.

Lutein and Zeaxanthin

These carotenoids of the xanthophyll family are most well-known health and protection defense against excessive blue light on the retina and oxidation. If you notice, these nutrients are relatively new to mainstream knowledge of nutrition. My humble opinion is that it is a new deficiency caused by our new world of staring into computer screens daily on top of the blue lit world that we live in; the Sun has always been here and will never go away. According to NCBI's website (Lutein and Zeaxanthin and their Role in Age-Related Macular Degeneration):

> *(Begin modified excerpt) The synthesis of these compound through consumption is low (maybe great to load up on leafy greens). They are the only carotenoids that accumulate in the retina, particularly the macula; they are called macular pigments.*

Some vegetarian foods rich in Lutein and Zeaxanthin: Grean leafy vegetables, carrots,

Rutin

Rutin is a bioflavonoid that works well alongside vitamin C, due to their roles in vessel repair, particularly the fine ones in the eyes..
According to allaboutvision.com:

> (Begin Modified excerpt) Rutin is known to regulate blood flow and strengthen blood vessel walls (blood flow and capillary health are key for eye health). It is thought to protect against capillaries bursting in eyes. In studies, rutin (with forskolin) reduced eye pressure (glaucoma) in patients undergoing and preparing for surgery by an average of 20%.

Some rich foods in rutin are: teas (black particularly), buckwheat, apples, asparagus

Omega 3 Fatty Acids

Our eyes have the highest concentration of DHA with the brain next. DHA is the only lipid that can transform sunlight into electricity (chemical energy) and vice versa. Our eyes have the biggest job of transforming light in the body, with the brain next in line. This a major portion of our nerve/electrical system. This is another major protector of blue-spectrum light (drains DHA from the body) or exessive light.
According to a Science Direct article on DHA (Lipid Mediators):

> (Begin modified excerpt) DHA is continuously used for the biogenesis and maintenance of neuronal and photoreceptor membranes. This system is supported by the liver.

DHA is a very loaded nutrient in regards to what it does the in the eye, brain, nervous system, and body. It probably by far the most important on this list. It is well known than seafood (shellfish and fish, especially cold water ones) is has the highest concentration, grass fed animals, and arguably green whole foods (which would have to be converted-believed that humans can hardly do). If you live in cold areas or never go outside or live your life under mostly blue light, this one becomes more important.

Putting This All Together

Since vision is an essential sense, as they all are, improving it has the potential to improve the entire body. Light and dark sensing systems govern a huge amount of our bodies' biological programs. What I'm alluding to here is the importance of these light sensing systems, which aren't just in the eyes but throughout the whole body.

In the same way an athlete supplements their diet based on their energy, nutritions, and maintenance needs, our eyes have certain diets that are favorable to them. In the previous section, I gave you a list of nutrients and vitamins that are essential to eye maintenance, integrity, and health. In the same a way a bodybuilder would supplement extra protein to build raw muscle, these previously mentioned nutrients replenish and rebuild eyes to protect them from too much light in certain frequencies or excess intensities; many of these promote small-vessel blood circulation and their repair. This becomes more important when you talk about nerve and capillary-rich areas in the body like the eyes and extremities.

I say all that to recommend a raw shake/smoothie with season and region appropriate fruit, vegetables, and herbs to supplement not only your sungazing experience but also protect you from the artificial light, especially blue, that everyone just ignores and pretends like it's harmless. Master your vegetarian portion of your diet to understand the deep important world of light and biology dynamics in your life.

A last mention that is probably deeply important is the presence of seafood in our diets. This information becomes a point of contention for some. Some believe that omega-3 fatty acids/ DHA and other such lipids essential to eyes the brain can only be obtained through a seafood diet. Some believe that sufficient amounts can be obtained from grass-fed land animals. Some believe that sufficient amounts can be obtained from a vegetable-rich, green diet. My belief is that the truth is somewhere in the middle. Obviously, the entire world does not have the ability to eat the same diet. In some cases, they can't eat meat. In other cases, only meat and/or seafood is an option. Some people have access to it all. Environment likely play a key role in what is the most optimal diet that facilitates our bodies' light systems best.

CHAPTER 7: SUN GAZING'S HEALTH RISKS, PRECAUTIONS, AND MY OWN PERSONAL ISSUES

I've already talked some about what the general scientific public thinks about the eyes' tolerances to light. Overall, they consider sunlight to be difficult ally. However, they nearly completely ignore the ubiquitous artificial light that we bath in daily. Modern life is continuing to promote that we endure and ignore the artificial light while blocking out the sun. No one seems to want to address or really acknowledge it. I speak about artificial light because it's the top antagonist for humans using the sun. I'm saying it (or our abuse of it) is what increases the Sun's potential to harm. To reiterate an above point, blue light ruins eyes because of it being used in one concentrated spectrum (any time we choose), making life a constant blue-light gazing/eating event.

Unfortunately, the Sun and artificial light are married in modern life.

Possibility Of Vision Deterioration

In this section, I won't focus much on science/evidence but will share a lot of anecdotal information. The main reason why is because, for obvious reasons, objective sun gazing data is not readily available. Again, I've done it religiously for over six years. In the very beginning, I did the HRM method. Becoming impatient due to my astonishment and fascination with it, I abandoned this method after about three months in to do whatever felt right to me. For the next year and a half, I did about forty minutes a day average (way too much) with satisfying results. Around this time, I did move to a city (unnatural environment) from the countryside, which is important to note because it changes how your body deals with nature. So, my thoughts are that you should scale back more when you live in unnatural places. After those first two years, I went to get an eye exam to extend my driver's license' validity. My eye-doctor indicated through a scanned computer-photo that I had inflammation on my retina and asked me if I look at the sun. He said that he was surprised that I could see as well as I could, based on the condition that he saw of my eyes in the computer photo. At that time, my sight and health felt better than ever to me. My eyes and brain had become very sensitive to light and visual cues of any kind; I felt that I was performing better through what I was doing (not saying I was right).

From that point on, I was more systematic and practical about how I sun gazed. I did about fifteen minutes-average per day thereafter. I stayed religious about wearing blue-light blocking glasses inside, getting to bed before ten, and keeping lights off in my home. Two years later, I got a similar diagnosis from another doctor about my retina but just like before, I had no subjective issues with my vision at that time either.

On the beginning of year six, I began paying attention to my feet/nails and wanted them pretty and perfect, free from any fungal infections (athletes foot) or unsightliness. I'd had this issue for about decade and did not live in a tropical area where I could get sunlight on them daily to cure it. I decided (against my better judgement) to take the pharmaceutical drug route, which required up to a year of anti-fungal medication to rid myself of it. About a month after beginning the medication, I felt weird and my vision dramatically got noticeably poor in that short window of time. Due to the timing, I had very little doubt that the antifungal medication was responsible but I also knew that sun gazing was particularly dangerous to continue. So, whether it was a culmination of the years of haphazard sun gazing brought to a peak by medication side effects or not, I ended my sun gazing journey at about six years. I completely took six months off. Around this time, I had begun supplementing colloidal gold and others, which helped in my abrupt transition; it made me more sensitive to the sun (positively). I seemed to get more satisfaction from less of it. For the rest of the year, I sun gazed periodically and did it in an indirect way (see next section) where I looked slightly off to the side of the sun instead of directly at it.

Alternative Safer Methods Of Sun Gazing

I'll share here two safer alternative methods of sun gazing. They are simple, specific, and just as effective as the standard method. The first method is what I call 'red light sun gazing'. For this method, the idea is healing your eyes without any emphasis on powering/building the eyes or the nervous system. For this, you look directly at the sun and close your eyes, receiving the Sun only through your eye-lids. You only get infrared light (penetrates many inches below the skins surface) through your eye-lids. You may need longer sessions to get a desired effect from this method.

Safety concerns for these will be minimized to a great degree when you do sun gazing like this.

The next method, I call 'indirect sun gazing'. In this method, you get UV (interacts with body surfaces primarily, like the body's skin and the eye's cornea) and full spectrum Sun in a more natural safer way. To do these: ground yourself, face the Sun, put the Sun in your field of vision (you see it but aren't looking at it), sun gaze like this, focusing on a part of the sky other than the Sun. What this does is that it gives you access to full spectrum of sun through the eyes at a much lower intensity. It eliminates/minimizes concentrating the Sun's image on a single point on your retina. If the intensity is too strong, simply look at the sun further away from your vision's point of focus (aim sight at the sun but shoot vision outside the scope of your aim). If you do these on midday, you will almost be looking straight up into the sky.

The H R M Method

In the HRM method, it is advised (and I paraphrase) to do it at first sunrise or sunset beginning with five seconds, adding five second per sessions daily, until you reach a grand total of forty-five minutes. After the forty-five-minute limit has been reached, it is advised to abandon sun gazing and walk barefoot for forty-five minutes per day for nine months to discharge excessive energy from the body. Arrogantly, I ignored this outstanding wisdom. My reason was not because I have disregard for convention and conservatism but because I felt that it was a watered-down prepackage version, not authentic HRM. I simply didn't believe that this was what HRM followed; I thought it to be a commercial version of the real thing. You see, sun gazing is already an extremely questionable activity. People are concerned about it (for good reason) and try and protect other people from themselves. If you are a sun gazer, then I know that you are a free thinker, a critically thinker, and don't want people to think for you. But in all fairness, we need each other to see where we are blind or ignorant sometimes. Sun gazing is highly experimental just like diets and lifestyles. We come across new gurus every day that show us where we were going wrong and put us back on the path. We need those people. Oftentimes, the truth is usually somewhere in the middle.

Importance Of Grounding When Sun Gazing

I've done an entire chapter on grounding already. My belief is that grounding flushes the body of extraneous light energy to connect you to the Sun and air energies. Aside from the Sun and the Earth, there is an abundance of energy in between it and the Sun (much of it manmade and artificial). We are eating/absorbing it constantly. The Sun is an anode (positive) and the Earth is a cathode (negative). Our technology (along with its energy byproducts) is replacing and mixing into the Sun's energy field and we can't nourish ourselves from it. So, in order to get the cleanest connection from the Sun to the Earth, we must have an unobstructed connection to the Earth (grounding). Keep in mind that underground artificial energy sources disrupt this connection (awareness of where you ground is necessary).

People always say to ground but rarely tell you result of choosing not to. I feel that an ungrounded circuit (body to ground), makes it easier to overload on the sun. We are always within the jurisdiction of the Earth's magnetic field, therefore always receiving at least some its grounding effects. Nevertheless, there are levels to grounding just like everything else. Though I feel that I need to repeat this many more times to fully believe it myself, here is some anecdotal evidence that I got recently (late in my sun gazing journey): I have had inflammation symptoms (pain) in my body that I relieved in a couple of grounded sessions (standing feet to ground). I generally had always sun gazed ungrounded, on cement, or grounded through sitting on my butt. I hadn't been giving it the respect that it deserved. Through testing, comparing, and paying attention, I found that the standing on my feet seemed to be superior to sitting on my bottom. I am guessing that the abundance of nerves (highly electrically conductive) in the feet are a best circuit entry point for receiving the Earth's energy. I always ignored through ignorance the difference between standing and otherwise. But, I have already touched on this earlier in talking about the electropotentials of various body parts in comparison to others. So now, I'm not lazy when I sun gazed. I stand barefoot on some nice dirt or sand focusing my mind on the task at hand. We will talk about the mind in conjunction with sun gazing in chapter 9.

Icing Your Eyes

I have not done this much myself but I want to talk about it theoretically. If you recall in my cold adaptation chapter, ice does magnificent things to order our biology. Sun gazing is a mechanically and chemically exhausting activity and stressor to the body which requires patient adaptation and recovery. Icing body parts is phenomenal for healing overuse and disorder, enhancing healing and recovery speed. So in theory, this would be a great adjunct to sun gazing because it gives some of the energy guiding/ordering effects and also slows down biological chemical clocks (anywhere in the body). So, a bio-resource draining activity like sun gazing would definitely benefit from such an action. A cautious person would be wise to incorporate this before and/or after a session to speed adaptation and recovery. I wish I'd have been patient and wise enough to incorporate this all along.

Timing Your Sessions And Making Diaries

I've always timed my sessions. My primary reasons for doing so has been for consistency and associating durations with effectiveness. You want to definitely be systematic in such a speculative activity. The Sun's fluxes vary widely moment to moment and day to day. Taking notes on sessions and tracking would be wise. However, no matter what, paying attention to how you feel and being observant to any difference that you experience is a valuable strategy in maintaining and developing good intuition and monitoring your progress and safety. On some days, you may not be able to reach your goal; never force anything. Always listen to your body first! If you are not feeling it, don't force it.

A diary for your sun gazing sessions is a great idea for not only what I just mentioned above but for tuning into the insights that you get through sun gazing. A lot of the gifts and downloads that we get are discovered incidentally and accidentally. Writing is a powerful way to see what you have downloaded. Just scanning your mind for information is inferior to the momentum that writing creates. You don't have to write much. Just a couple of sentences per session is sufficient. You can write before, during, or immediately after; find what works best in your favor.

If I Could Do It All Over Again

If I could do it all over again, I would've done it in the HRM method. I would've built my nervous system gradually and carefully ground in the best places standing barefoot. You can learn a lot from a dummy! I'm your and my own dummy! I have had homeruns and strike-outs with this practice. I would not have jumped to long times too quickly as I did. Patience is definitely a virtue with this practice. I think that this practice could be evolved far beyond what HRM recommended but I think that his recommended procedure should be utilized first before advancing into the more untested areas. I would have never done hour-plus sessions or do peak-sun hours before my first two years of training (I did peak sun hours a lot in my second half of the six years). I recommend consistently taking vision tests (even simple vision tests) right from the beginning on a regular basis to assess for any negative trends. If you have access, get high quality technological eye scans to assess for diminishing and recuperative functions of your eyes. If complications arise, you can always scale back what you are doing, for example, earlier sunrises and shorter sessions or more days in between for recovery. It is a highly individual endeavor.

At this point of writing, I have no problematic issues with my eyes (my vision has never been great) but I feel that I could have actually built better eyes and body by taking heed to the above. It is why I write this book, to let you stand on my shoulders. The mainstream is not going to do it any time soon.

CHAPTER 8: WATER HACKS: MY FAVORITES AND WHY

Magnetizing And Structuring Your Water

Water is a magnetic dipole, meaning that it can align its crystal molecules to magnetic fields. As we've talked about already, structure in water facilitates energy conduction/use. It enables the Sun to transfer more energy to biological tissues when it is organized. The Earth's magnetic field has organizing effects on water but you can order your own drinking water more by putting it in a strong local magnetic field for an hour or longer. The poles of the magnet have differing effects on water. The topic of biology and magnetism is speculative, even though there are great books out on the topic. The most commonly accepted wisdom/belief on the topic is that the north-seeking pole of the magnet has a calming effect, while the south-seeking pole has more of a stimulating effect on the body. I can attest to north-seeking magnet's healing properties over the south-seeking side's excitatory properties; my experiences support this. However, in simply magnetizing water (not a body), I can't speak on well at all.

Water consumption alone increases metabolism significantly. Not all water is the same; there are levels to water. Some water that you drink can be lower energy, for example when you add electronegative elements like fluoride to it. Water has memory and retains information from the environments that it has been in. Moving/running water has more energy than stationary water. Cold water is more ordered, thereby giving you a greater energy boost than the opposite. In cold winters, the sun is usually weaker. So to compensate, the cold environments provide more organized well-structured water to drink.

To give you more tangible explanations of how different ordered water is over unstructured water, magnetize a glass of water and compare it to an un-magnetized one. What you will notice is that the magnetized water is a lot wetter and smoother to drink, has a thinner texture to it (think of water absorbing into versus beading up on a surface and not absorbing). Magnetizing water shrinks the molecules of water allowing them to do more work, probably due to it having more surface area. Another test you can do to understand the difference between the two, is add soap to it and clean something. Washing with magnetized water is far easier and effortless to do than regular water; it does more work with less effort. Magnetized water is far more penetrable to the body than other water, which I'm sure is attributable to it increased bioavailability. If you want to get more nutrition and hydration out of your drinks (I love magnetized wine), magnetized them before you drink.

Copper Water

Copper is a good mineral to modestly add to water. It is easy to add due to how easily it leeches from pots (pure copper) to water stored in them. An overnight storage of water in a copper pot should be enough to get a sufficient dose into your drinking water. Copper is a very high-electron metal, making it highly conductive (think about copper wires being common in electricity use). Photons are only attracted to electrons. Higher electron sources definitely have an affinity for the Sun. Copper can increase the conductivity of water. It can kill most pathogens in water in a short amount of time. It definitely turns your water on.

As for copper as a bio-mineral, it is one of the most important in the body. Having a deficiency will definitely show you how important it is. Most of the body's functions require copper to facilitate them. One of the most interesting uses of copper to me in the body is its role in making melanin. Melanin is an important mysterious product in the skin triggered primarily by UV light exposure. It is what gives skin colors and tans. Melanin is a major component in the eyes' dealing with Sun or its excess! Melanin is far more than just nature's sunblock. The skin is a solar panel that takes the Sun and converts it to electricity. Melanin is equivalent to chlorophyll in plants, in that it can take the energy of the Sun and convert it to electricity for the body. For me, something is missing in the vitamin D narrative where it is suggested that darker skin lowers (blood observable) vitamin D. Although this may be true, I feel that the added properties of melanin accounts for (or compensates for) the lower test number's health implications. I feel that melanin discoveries will break open possibilities for the body's potentials and health in the future.

Copper leeched into water has good bioavailability. Vitamins often lack this. For someone fixing a deficiently, high copper foods have great bioavailability. With that said, copper can be easy to overdo; and the side effects are similar to that of deficiencies. Copper is not something that you want to intentionally take too much of. However, many people figure that they need more. If you feel or want to have more copper safely, the transdermal route is great because the skin is very selective about what it lets in and out of the body. Simply rub copper water onto your skin instead of drinking.

Sun Charged Water

Sun-charged water is where you put your water out in the Sun to receive and store its energy. The UV and Infrared light from the sun are the most energy relevant light from the Sun when charging water. To Sun charge water, the Sun needs to shine directly into it, not through some material like glass or plastic. Many materials block out various spectrums of light, for example, glass blocks UV but quartz does not. Once water is ordered and optionally mineralized, it can be energized well with the Sun. Of course, some use artificial light to charge water but sunlight is definitely superior. Crystals can be added to water to enhance the charging. I can't recommend a best or great crystal to use at this time.

Sun charged and treated water are great additions and substitutes for cosmetic skin care. Doing so gives you a living-cosmetic working with the sun, versus an artificial one blocking the sun and irritating your skin.

CHAPTER 9: ESOTERIC CONNECTIONS AND SUN GAZING

Astrological Portals

Sun gazing introduced me to the sky and astrology. My initial obsession with the Sun guided me into doing more research about what the Sun is and was. There are the ancient fables/myths, the physical and biological scientific information, the observations of its patterns, and the connection that it has with our lives on a spiritual level. Sun gazing lead me down all of these interesting roads. Its cleansing and purifying properties connected me closer to "my higher self". I could feel and see more, therefore becoming more curious about everything. It is definitely a door to the so called "woo-woo world". Embrace your "crazy". Make sure it is actually "crazy" first before you dismiss it.

So, let's talk a little "woo-woo". In astrology, the Sun predicts, explains, and guides us on topics like our ego, life purpose, self-expression, and how we focus our attention. In respects to clairvoyance, sun gazing sessions can have a spectrum of different manifestation powers at any given time. Certain manifestations are more/less effective at certain times. Learning about these windows can help you become more efficient in how you use this time. For example, on your birthday, check the moon's phase. If the moon is waxing (growing bigger), you have greater manifestation power to bring things into your life for that year; if waning (growing smaller), you can more easily remove things from your life for that year. The bigger/smaller the moon is, the greater the manifestation power for that year. Each moon phase has its own momentum. Find out what that phases represents and see if you feel it is worthy of you seeding specific manifestations for on that year.

To get more specific on these, you'd have to know your astrology well or be guided by someone who does. As you sun gaze, take that portal's energy in knowingly and apply your own mind's intentions. Don't just let your sun gazing session be a physical mechanical experience. Use your intention's powers and summon as many answers to your questions as you can. Avoid going into a sun gazing session with an empty purpose. Don't ever sun gaze just to look at the Sun or purely to build your health. Accomplish as much as you can and have new goals every session. It's a powerful time limited by you.

Watch your mood and temperament when you sun gaze. Although the Sun facilitates your body in making mood enhancing chemicals and hormones, it can super-charge feelings (feelings are very real and ready for manifestation). Don't feed such an internal situation. Either empty your mind meditatively before you begin, or skip that day and start over on another happier day. Consider doing something else that day like taking a grounded walk.

Numerological Connections And Spiritual Windows

On March 13, 2022, Hira Ratan Manek died at the age of 85. He is not my initial motivator for beginning but my initial motivation for believing in the power of the Sun and its potential. I didn't learn of his passing until January 2023. At that time, I was surprised that he'd been dead that long without me catching it on any media platform. Something that I immediately realized was that his death date overlapped my separation from sun gazing due to complication with the antifungal medication (I talked about in chapter 7). I recalled that I just could not get back into it for the remainder of 2022. I found it really odd how in a five-plus year committed habit, I suddenly just lost desire for it. So, what I'm getting at here is that I feel there is definitely an aspect of divinity and guidance for all of us. Listen and pay attention to the signs, learning how to read into and as deeply beneath the surface as you can. Think on your own but allow others' points of view to guide you when you are not fully confident in your own discernment. We are one.

Another coincidence (or not) was that I am a life path number six in numerology (add birth year numerals, birth month numerals, and birthday numerals to a single digit). Life path number six people tend to be destined for a life related to compassion, teaching, guiding, healing, peace-keeping, and more. My sun gazing journey (approximately six years of dedication) ended (discontinued for the first time) on this sixth year. I am writing about it now because I feel like I have collected enough data about my whole experience to share it coherently, articulately, and insightfully. I write this book as my own reference and because I wish that someone would have had it written for me when I took my first steps on this journey.

Meditations And Mind Work

There are countless mediations that can be done in conjunction with this. I will share a few of them that I have done.

1. Ask questions, not at the Sun but to yourself (or your spirit guides). Patiently and confidently look and wait for the answers that you asked for. If you don't believe or are skeptical, it is better to not ask the question at all (your skepticism will just confuse you).

2. Follow the light through your body as you receive it. Take ti to places that you want nourished, healed, or strengthened. As they say, where your attention goes, energy flows. Avoid having a dormant mind while doing this, unless you are intentionally emptying it.

3. Begin sessions with affirmations and shows of gratitude. Share as much as you can about what you are proud of in your life or about other people in the world.

4. Utilise the Akashic records. Look/focus inside. Ask you masters (this is up to you to decide) to collaborate with you. Ask the question or set out the intention (for you or someone else). When finished, thank your masters and greet them in a departure.

THANKS FOR READING!

Please Be Sure to Rate this Book Here.

Below are My Other Books (My Genres Vary)

<u>Science Fiction</u>

Lifetimes of a Mars Breakaway Unit: Space Travel, Reincarnation, and Universe Mysteries

<u>Romance, Drama, Adventure</u>

Love, Lust & Border: Foreign Romances, Vices, and Life Transformations

<u>Biography/Sports</u>
A Fighter's Diary: Why Boxers (Fighters) are Special

Find Me on YouTube
https://www.youtube.com/@Zene369/videos

Made in the USA
Las Vegas, NV
04 October 2023

78574688R00039